IMAGES
of America

RIDGEFIELD

The sidewalk on the east side of Main Street, just south of the Keeler Tavern Museum, still has a curve, and many of these ancient trees are still standing.

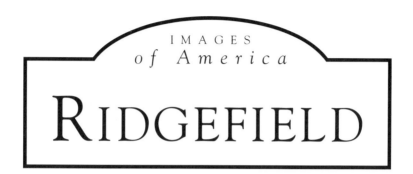

IMAGES
of America

RIDGEFIELD

Ridgefield Archives Committee

ARCADIA

Published by Arcadia Publishing,
an imprint of Tempus Publishing, Inc.
2 Cumberland Street
Charleston, SC 29401

Printed in Great Britain.

Library of Congress Catalog Card Number: 99-63938

For all general information contact Arcadia Publishing at:
Telephone 843-853-2070
Fax 843-853-0044
E-Mail edit@arcadiaimages.com

For customer service and orders:
Toll-Free 1-888-313-BOOK

Visit us on the internet at http://www.arcadiaimages.com

The "old watering trough," donated to the town by novelist and *Life Magazine* publisher John Ames Mitchell, is shown here *c.* 1910. It originally stood at Main and Catoonah Streets (above). This view looks west up Catoonah Street, with the Methodist church and the firehouse at right. Mitchell specified that the trough serve not only horses, but wandering dogs—hence, the opening at the bottom. The trough now stands in the triangle of West and Olmstead Lanes, where it is used as a big flower pot in the summer. Mitchell lived at "Windover" on West Lane nearly opposite Silver Spring Road.

CONTENTS

The Hauley house, built in 1714 for the first minister of the Congregational Church, still stands as a private residence opposite the town green, at the corner of Branchville Road and Main Street.

INTRODUCTION

". . . that kind of beauty which consists in blending
the peace and quietude of cultivated valleys
with the sublimity of mountains . . ."

—Samuel G. Goodrich Jr. (Peter Parley), August 20, 1855

Settlers from Norwalk, Connecticut, wishing to establish a new community in the undeveloped northern land, created Ridgefield, Connecticut, founded in 1708, from the Connecticut wilderness near the New York State border. They purchased 22,399 acres, an area 10 miles long and about 5 miles wide, from the Ramapoo Indians. On a ridge of this beautiful high land the proprietors laid out Ridgefield's Main Street. The 25 "lotts" still exist and still form one of the loveliest Main Streets in Connecticut. Lot No. 5 was reserved for the first minister of this Congregational Church community. The first church was built on Main Street, across from the home built in 1714 for Reverend Thomas Hauley (the house still bears his name). In 1769, Ridgebury, the northernmost section of Ridgefield, established its own church to serve those who settled 8 miles north of the town center.

A small inland community of several thousand souls, Ridgefield grew slowly, providing shelter and sustenance for its own. Millers, tanners, shoemakers, blacksmiths, and taverns that offered meals and a night's lodging fulfilled the needs of Ridgefielders and visitors alike.

Although Ridgefielders took part in every war in this land's history, it is the Revolutionary War that struck closest to home. The war came to Ridgefield on April 27, 1777, when British troops, under the command of Gen. William Tryon, were attacked by the rebels as they were returning to Westport after destroying American supplies stored in Danbury, to the north. American Gen. David Wooster was mortally wounded in a brief skirmish along the way. The Americans erected a barricade on north Main Street, and under the command of Gen. Benjamin Silliman and Gen. Benedict Arnold, fought the British in what history remembers as the Battle of Ridgefield. Arnold's horse was shot out from under him, but he survived to become America's best-known traitor. The British proceeded south on Main Street, firing at what they considered rebel homes. A British cannonball still remains embedded in a corner post of the Keeler Tavern Museum (Lot No. 2).

The quiet rural existence of Ridgefield was disrupted almost a century later by the Civil War, when young men enlisted in the armies of the North. When the war was over, the town began

In 1908, during the town's bicentennial celebration, it was written: "There is no fairer scene in Connecticut than Ridgefield's Main Street, a mile or more of fine houses and velvety lawns, shaded by great elms and maples. Cool, restful shadows, songs of birds, glimpses of sunny fields attract and charm the visitor, beguiling him into a fancy that this is some lovely old world park rather than the thoroughfare of a New England Village."

to lose population. The rocky land was never ideal for farming, and many of its young men left for the superior farmland to the west. Ridgefield did not have a large river to create the waterpower to drive a mill, and so the Industrial Revolution passed it by. The small town, built on high ridges, was then discovered by wealthy New Yorkers who were looking for a healthy place to build their summer homes and escape from the heat and noise of the city.

The "summer people" built large estates requiring many servants (often Irish immigrants) and estate managers who, with their families, settled in town. Many of the wealthy families were active in publishing, banking, and the arts. When summer was over they left Ridgefield and returned to Manhattan. Their interest in Ridgefield, however, continued throughout the winter. Many served on town and church boards, and were instrumental in improving the amenities of the town. In a very real sense the "summer people" gave new life to Ridgefield, as they provided inspiration and financial assistance toward better water, sewer, and electrical systems. A wave of Italian immigrants arrived to provide the manpower to build these new systems. They and their families settled here and soon became an influential part of the community.

Ridgefield remained unchanged until after World War II, when many corporations and businesses moved out of New York City to suburban areas. This enabled commuters to live in Ridgefield and travel to their jobs in surrounding towns, as well as New York City. Many of the old estates were sold and subdivided, but much still remains of early Ridgefield. The proprietors did choose well.

—Ridgefield Archives Committee
Ridgefield, Connecticut

One

EARLY HISTORY

Ridgefield's history was first visually recorded by drawings, which are found in the early histories of the town. Many of these illustrations give the flavor of the era before the advent of photography. The site of the Battle of Ridgefield was popular, and after the development of photography, many photographs were taken of this location, as well as other important sites, buildings, and major events. One of the most frequently photographed buildings is what is now the Keeler Tavern Museum. This c. 1714 farmhouse, which in 1772 became an inn and stagecoach stop, was shot at with a barrage of cannonballs during the battle. A cannonball remains in a corner post of the building. After the Battle of Ridgefield, which occurred on April 27, 1777, the great fire of December 1895 was probably the most traumatic event to occur in town. Many buildings in the village district were destroyed that night. Downtown Ridgefield rose from the ashes as a new century dawned.

The Stebbins house, right, served as a hospital and morgue for casualties of the battle. Its hearthstone, carved with the date 1727, can still be found on the property, now the location of the Casagmo condominiums. The buttery door, scarred during the battle, is on display at the Keeler Tavern Museum.

North Main Street is shown here in the early 1800s. From left to right are the Stebbins house, at the site of the Battle of Ridgefield; the Gilbert home, which remains a private residence at 536 Main Street; a small house that is today part of the Elms Inn and Restaurant at 500 Main Street; and the 18th-century Rockwell home, which is now the Elms Restaurant and Tavern at 500 Main Street.

10

Benjamin Stebbins, a tanner from Massachusetts, was encouraged by his friend, Reverend Thomas Hauley, to come to Ridgefield. He arrived in 1714 and was granted a rocky plot of land at the head of the main street by the proprietors in 1721. Six years later he built his house, which stood on the site until it was demolished at the turn of the century to make way for the palatial home of George M. Olcott.

Miss Mary Olcott, the daughter of George Olcott, erected this battle monument in the wall of the Casagmo property. It marks the nearby site of mass graves of both American and British soldiers who died on that fateful April day in 1777.

Gen. Benedict Arnold, then still a great American hero, led the patriots against the British in the bloody conflict. He narrowly escaped death when his horse was shot out from under him at the barricade. The enemy continued its march through the town, firing along the way at known patriot buildings. A controversial medal in honor of General Arnold was issued in 1977 for the 200th anniversary of the Battle of Ridgefield.

American Gen. David Wooster was killed while leading a small group of patriots in pursuit of the British troops. A monument to his memory can be seen on North Salem Road. The group's bravery gave the Americans time to prepare the barricade being erected further south across Main Street.

This photograph from the 1860s, showing only one gable and one dormer window, is the earliest known image of the Keeler Tavern. Originally the Benjamin Hoyt house on Lot No. 2, it was passed down by marriage through the Hoyt and Keeler families, and eventually to Anna Keeler and her husband, Abijah Resseguie.

The cannonball shot by the British into the corner post of the north façade of the Keeler Tavern can still be seen by visitors to the museum.

Abijah Ressiguie, known as an amiable landlord and great storyteller, is seen standing in front of the entrance to his hotel in the late 1800s. Landlord Ressiguie, of Huguenot descent, was a man of great character and strength, and was greatly loved in the community.

Abijah Resseguie is shown in this photograph of the northern side of the inn in front of the piazza that had been a part of the house for many years. It was removed during a renovation in the 1960s.

14

The Peter Parley house on High Ridge was originally built in 1797 for Samuel Goodrich Sr., the third minister of the Congregational Church. It is named after his son, Samuel Goodrich Jr., who wrote under the pen name of Peter Parley. Preston Bassett, a well-known inventor and historian, lived in the Peter Parley house for many years. It remains a private residence.

Samuel Goodrich Jr., an accomplished writer and successful publisher, is shown in silhouette. His *Recollections of a Lifetime*, published in 1856, contains more than 100 pages describing growing up in Ridgefield, as well as an account of his return to Ridgefield after an absence of nearly 50 years.

The Nathan Scott homestead, one of Ridgefield's earliest homes, was built on the original Lot No. 13. In 1922 the building was moved from Main Street around the corner to Catoonah Street, to make room for a new commercial building. As it is again in the way of progress, the fate of the venerable old Scott house is in doubt.

According to writer Peter Parley, who attended the West Lane schoolhouse in the early 19th century, the building was "unpainted, made of rough boards and a stone chimney, so big that the rain and snow fell upon the hearth . . . A very old chestnut tree stood at the western angle, and in those days was the only shade." This view shows a much improved version of the schoolhouse c. 1910.

16

Having spent just under 50 years using the first floor of the Masonic Hall (barely visible at right) for meetings and other community use, the town erected a new town hall on the lot next door. Costing $6,000 in 1876, the building was to be used for only nineteen years as, in 1895, it was destroyed in the fire that devastated the downtown area.

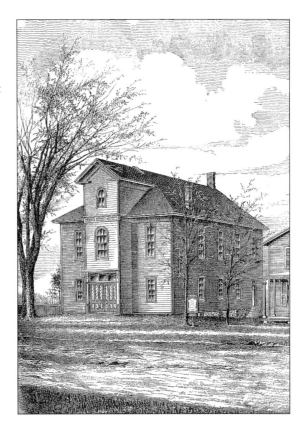

The Barhite & Valden General Store is shown here in the early 1890s. Located north of the Bedient Block, it was to suffer a similar fate when it, and the Western Union office next door, burned to the ground in the fire.

RIDGEFIELD CENTER BEFORE
THE GREAT FIRE OF 1895
☐ BUILDINGS BURNED TO THE GROUND

It took just six hours one cold winter's evening to reduce a section of Main Street to smoldering ruins. On December 8, 1895, around 9:00 p.m., a passerby saw flames coming out of the Gage building, which housed Bedient & Mead, an undertaking and furniture store. Church bells sounded the alarm, and hundreds arrived to form a bucket brigade to fight the blaze On Bailey

Ridgefield, having no organized fire department, requested help from Danbury, but by the time the train carrying the men and equipment arrived at 3 a.m., the fire had almost burned out.

18

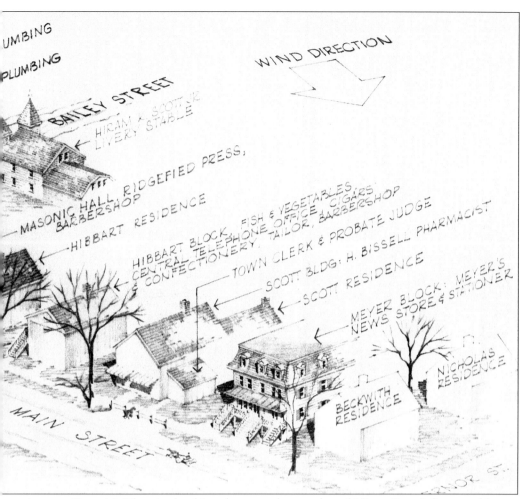

UMBING

PLUMBING

WIND DIRECTION

BAILEY STREET

HIRAM A. SCOTT'R
LIVERY STABLE

MASONIC HALL RIDGEFIELD PRESS,
BARBERSHOP

HIBBART RESIDENCE

HIBBART BLOCK, FISH & VEGETABLES,
CENTRAL TELEPHONE OFFICE, CIGARS,
& CONFECTIONERY, TAILOR, BARBERSHOP

TOWN CLERK & PROBATE JUDGE

SCOTT BLDG; H. BISSELL PHARMACIST

SCOTT RESIDENCE

MEYER BLOCK; MEYER'S
NEWS STORE & STATIONER

NICHOLAS
RESIDENCE

BECKWITH
RESIDENCE

MAIN STREET

NOR ST.

Avenue, Peter McGlynn's plumbing shop was destroyed, and Hiram Scott's livery stable was damaged. Soon the town hall was engulfed in flames. The fire spread southward on Main Street destroying everything up to and including the Scott Block. Sparks and wind also threatened buildings on the western side of Main Street, but small fires were quickly extinguished.

The glow from the fire could be seen in the sky for miles around, and the following day curious visitors came to view the scene. Damage was estimated at nearly $100,000, which was largely covered by insurance.

As a result of the devastation, improvements that had been called for in past years were finally begun, the most important of which was the organization of the Ridgefield Volunteer Fire Department on February 10, 1897.

Two

THE MAIN ATTRACTION: MAIN STREET

In 1896 Ridgefield began to rise from the ashes of the devastating fire. Buildings constructed of brick and stone replaced the old wooden structures, street lighting was improved, new roads were built, and old roads were upgraded. These changes brought new faces to the community. Stone masons from the Ancona region in Italy arrived to construct a new sewer system, and to lay pipes bringing a much-needed water supply to the business district. A new brick town hall (above), built at a cost of $16,000, housed town offices and an auditorium that accommodated community events for many years.

Town Hall, Ridgefield, Conn.

A completed town hall, now covered with English ivy, stands in place of the small wooden building. The tall door on the side of the building was used for fire apparatus for the newly formed fire department, housed on the bottom floor of the building.

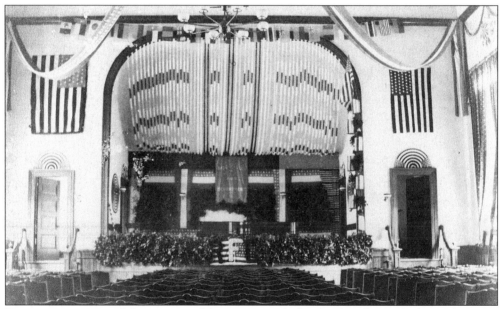

Few pictures remain of the interior of the new town hall. The first floor, which was for many years an open area, was the scene of town meetings as well as basketball games, high school plays, band concerts, and other community events. In later years, when the building was remodeled, the auditorium and stage were removed and replaced with offices.

22

The Jerusalem Lodge No. 49, AF&AM (Ancient Free and Accepted Masons), was chartered on October 25, 1808. The original hall, built in 1817, was destroyed in the fire of 1895, but was rebuilt a year later on the same site, part of the original Lot No. 11.

Women of the Order of the Eastern Star are shown here with members of their male counterpart, the Masons. Rockwell, Gilbert, Selleck, Scott, Hartmann and Knapp are some of the familiar names of members who appear in this Hartmann photograph, taken around the turn of the 20th century.

Two views looking north from the corner of Bailey Avenue show how little Main Street changed in the first quarter century after the fire. The view below shows the watering trough in the middle of the street that allowed horses to quench their thirst after traveling along the dusty roads.

Main Street looks the same many years later, only the names of the stores have changed. It's been a long time since snow blanketed the streets as deeply as it did when this photograph was taken in the 1920s.

The sign in the window of Willis Gilbert's shoe store on Main Street reads: "Up-to-date shoes." Abby Gilbert, Willis' daughter, is standing on the steps of the store.

Main Street was still a dirt road, and automobiles had not yet replaced horse-drawn wagons, when this photograph was taken of the east side of Main Street. The only changes in the image below seem to be the absence of the horse and the preponderance of autos. Long before disease destroyed the American Elm, these majestic trees lined the main street. One longtime resident remembers driving down the dirt road in his father's wagon in the summertime, with the elms making a leafy, green canopy overhead. He has never forgotten the beauty of the scene.

This building is easily recognized as the present Roma Block. Back in the early part of the 20th century, Francis Martin established his jewelry and optometrist business on the first floor. Mr. Martin, shown below on the right, became an influential figure in town. His business was purchased by the Craig family in 1949 and continues today at a location further south.

Shown here after a snowstorm is the Odd Fellows Hall on Main Street, built by the fraternal organization in 1928. The IOOF, Pilgrim Lodge No. 46, was established in Ridgefield in 1847, meeting in the Masonic Hall until 1895, when that building was destroyed in the Great Fire. This hall was one of the most popular spots in Ridgefield during the 1930s and '40s for music and dancing. In 1956 the IOOF sold the building and moved to the carriage house of the old Freund estate on King Lane. The building at 441 Main Street currently houses stores.

The Amos Smith Tavern was built on the corner of Main and Prospect Streets in 1797, and served the community for many years as both tavern and meeting hall. In the early years of the 20th century it was razed to make way for the new library building.

The first library in Ridgefield was established in 1795. For the next 100 years it was housed in several locations throughout the town. The growing library needed additional space, so plans were made to purchase land from the descendants of the Smith family. In 1901 James N. Morris had the new library built in memory of his deceased wife, Elizabeth W. Morris.

An early picture of the library interior shows what is now the history room, looking beyond the foyer into the present reading room.

Today the building looks the same, but the gardens behind it are gone, replaced by a building that was first a movie theater and then a bank. Looking east in the photograph below, past the library and down Prospect Street, the railroad station is visible at the bottom of the hill. A spur line from the Danbury-Norwalk line in Branchville was built in 1870, making travel much easier into Ridgefield, and bringing with it a new wave of visitors.

The earliest known picture of the train station is shown above. Later the yard, handsomely paved and graveled, was filled with smart equipages, phaetons, surreys, buggies, and wagons. Coachmen in colorful livery sounded their horns as they awaited the train from Grand Central Station, ready to drive the commuters to their "cottages." The station still exists as a warehouse of Ridgefield Supply.

Before the spur line was built, the train service from New York stopped at the station in Branchville. Horse-drawn carriages would taxi people up the winding hills to the village, to the many inns and hotels located throughout town. A popular destination was the Elm Shade Cottages shown here.

John Rockwell, seen on the front porch with his family, opened the Elm Shade Cottages to lodgers in 1860. The property continues to serve the community as an inn and restaurant.

Hiram B. Scott sold his popular drugstore to Harvey P. Bissell in 1895, four months before the building was destroyed in the Great Fire. Rebuilt in 1896 and opened under the name of Harvey P. Bissell, the building is shown here decorated for the bicentennial in 1908. Harvey Bissell was prominent in politics throughout his life. Bissell's Drug Store is still in business and shares the first floor with Gail's Station House restaurant.

This postcards view looks north from the corner of Main and Governor Streets. The First National Bank is visible on the right; beyond it is a house owned by Mrs. William Griffin that contained businesses on the lower two levels and apartments above. It was taken down in 1930 to make way for the new offices of the Ridgefield Savings Bank, now the Ridgefield Bank.

When Gov. Phineas Lounsbury acquired the old Dr. Perry place, he named it Grovelawn and made it his home for several years. He eventually decided to build a new home on the same site, and had this house moved to a piece of land on the property, adjacent to a footpath leading up the hill to East Ridge.

The old Grovelawn can been seen on the left in this postcard view. The building still stands, although greatly altered, and the road is now Governor Street.

Governor Lounsbury and his family are seen on the porch of Grovelawn, his grand new home. It was modeled after the Connecticut State building, which he had seen at the 1893 Columbian Exposition in Chicago. It took a staff of 14 to maintain the house, and 12 for the grounds. Louis Martin, father of the late Francis Martin, was the estate manager.

Photographer Joseph Hartmann took this springtime view looking toward East Ridge showing the back of the Lounsbury property. The large house on the left, then the home of George L. Rockwell, now houses the Ridgefield Police Department. Unchanged except for the windmill, the third house from the left is the home of Mr. and Mrs. Michael Manning. Sue Manning served as first selectman for many years.

The Hurlbutt meat market (on the left) was established by David Hurlbutt (1801–1858) during the early part of the 19th century. Sereno Hurlbutt, David's son, is leaning against the fence in front of his home. The house at 304 Main Street, which was for many years the home of Laura Curie Allee Shields, has recently undergone significant remodeling and restoration.

In 1783, Lt. Joshua King, a hero of the Revolution, and partner William Dole established their mercantile business in this little building that was to become known as Old Hundred. When the business was moved, Old Hundred became a private home. The building was jacked up and a new first floor was added. Fashion designer and art collector Lawrence Aldrich purchased the property in 1963, and today it is the Aldrich Museum of Contemporary Art at 258 Main Street.

In 1907, Cass Gilbert, a distinguished New York architect, bought the Ressiguie Hotel from Anna Marie Ressiguie to be used as his summer home. Respecting the original structure, he added a gambrel-roofed ell to provide space for family and social life, and for servants quarters.

Mr. and Mrs. Cass Gilbert are seated on the north terrace in 1928. The others are, from left to right, as follows: (front row) grandchildren Charlie and Grosvenor Gilbert, Judy Post, Cass Gilbert III, and Jarvis Gilbert; (back row) son-in-law Charles M. Post, daughters Julia Post and Emily, daughter-in-law Jarvis Gilbert, and Cass Gilbert Jr.

With this elegant garden house, a walled garden, and landscaped grounds, the Gilberts turned the simple farm-like Keeler Tavern/Resseguie Hotel into a gracious country home. In deference to its history Cass Gilbert named it the Cannonball House.

In 1915 a decision was made by the town to accept Cass Gilbert's offer of a marble fountain to be placed at West Lane and Main Street, rather than a proposed watering trough. The fountain, designed by Mr. Gilbert in a simple classical style, has become a landmark and a much-loved symbol of the town.

Three

A HISTORICAL
FOCUS ON FAITH

Religious faith was an integral part of the Ridgefield community from its founding, and it remains so today as new congregations have enriched the life of the town. In Ridgefield's first 200 years, five congregations were established. The town, laid out in 1708 in a simple straightforward manner, had "lotts" around a central common. The Congregational Meeting House stood on the common, and was the site of worship, town government, and education. On the east side of the street opposite the meetinghouse was the home of the first minister, Rev. Thomas Hauley. A second meetinghouse was completed in 1800, and was used until 1888, when the present stone church at the intersection of Main Street and West Lane was completed and dedicated. In this unknown artist's painting looking south along Main Street from King Lane, the Hauley house is pictured on the left with the second meetinghouse on the green in the distance.

This view of the second meetinghouse of the Congregational Church, on the town green opposite Branchville Road, shows the more elaborate steeple with a cupola that, in 1817, replaced the original structure. Fifty-eight feet long and forty feet wide, this meetinghouse was renovated and refurbished several times during its use from 1800 until July 15, 1888.

This photograph shows the interior of the second meetinghouse as it was when the last services were held before the structure was removed.

The new stone church at West Lane and Main Street was built on land donated by descendents of Rev. Jonathon Ingersoll, the second pastor, and dedicated on July 18, 1888. J. Cleveland Cady, a summer resident, designed the church after a small Italian church he had seen during his travels. The clock and chimes are a memorial to J. Howard King, the great-grandson of Reverend Ingersoll.

A later view looking west shows lush ivy on the walls of the church. The Ridgefield Club, further down West Lane, was purchased by the church in 1917, and remained in use until it was destroyed by fire in 1978. The building housed an auditorium, a stage, and a bowling alley, along with several meeting rooms. The intersection of Main Street and West Lane shows the triangle before the Cass Gilbert fountain was placed there.

Organized originally in 1742 as the New Patent Meeting House (named after the area purchased from local Native Americans in 1731), the small Ridgebury congregation built its first church in 1760 and secured its first resident minister in 1769.

In 1851 the present-day Ridgebury Congregational Church was erected on the same site, the west corner of Ridgebury Road, opposite George Washington Highway.

Early Church of England members in Ridgefield first gathered for worship in 1725, and in 1740 a church was built on land granted by the town proprietors. After the congregation disbanded during Revolutionary War fervor, the building was used to store Patriot supplies, and was burned by the British. A second church was built after the war, and in 1839 the congregation constructed the renamed St. Stephen's Episcopal Church.

Consecrated in 1916, the stone church, which still serves the congregation, occupies the same site as the earlier church buildings on Main Street. At the St. Stephen's 250th anniversary communion service in 1975, the deacons used the congregation's original prayer book, which was printed in London in 1742, as well as authentic colonial chalices.

Meeting first in 1787 and organized formally in 1790, the Methodist congregation worshiped in private homes for several years. The first church was built at the fork of North Salem Road and North Street, and was replaced by a white frame church built at Main and Catoonah Streets in 1841. In 1883 this small church was moved back on the site, remodeled, and renamed. In the 1960s the building was razed and a new one was built on the old town green at the intersection of Main Street and Branchville Road.

The remodeled church building was rededicated as the Jesse Lee Methodist Church, honoring an illustrious and inspiring Methodist circuit rider who preached in Ridgefield in the late 1700s. Mrs. Horace Walker is shown here on the steps of the church with her Sunday school class around 1922.

As Catholic families began moving into Ridgefield in the mid-1800s, masses were celebrated in parishioners' homes. In 1879 the first church was built at the eastern end of Catoonah Street. It was enlarged in 1888 as membership increased. The building, now the home of the Thrift Shop, was still not large enough to serve the congregation, so it was sold and plans were undertaken for a new and larger church.

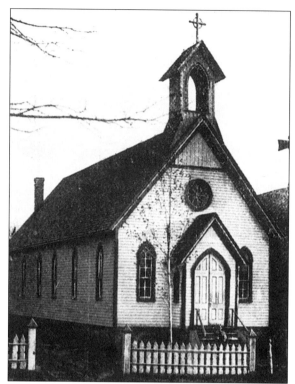

In 1896 the cornerstone was laid for the new church on 2.25 acres of land at the corner of Catoonah Street and High Ridge Avenue. In the cornerstone were placed items of parish, town and national concern, copies of the *Ridgefield Press* and the *Irish World*, as well as other items of interest. The new St. Mary's Church was dedicated in 1897 and continues to serve the parish.

It wasn't until September 1901 that the steeple bell was installed in the new church, and it tolled for the first time on September 14, 1901, when word was received that President William McKinley had died of wounds from an assassin's bullet. The handsome Victorian rectory next to the church was completed in 1894 and razed in 1974.

This turn-of-the-20th-century photograph by Hartmann shows Reverend Richard E. Shortell in his carriage, being pulled by his horse, Peggy. It was during Father Shortell's 41-year tenure as pastor, from 1893 until his death in 1934, that the church, the rectory, and the clubhouse across the street were erected. Significant church groups were also founded during this period, including the Knights of Columbus.

Four

HAMLETS AND NEIGHBORHOODS

As Ridgefield developed, there were three distinguishable hamlets: Titicus, Ridgebury, and Branchville. Titicus is the area around the intersection of North Salem, Mapleshade, and Saw Mill Hill Roads. The Russell home (shown here), known today as the 1735 Epenetus Howe house, still stands at 91 North Salem Road. It had a sign in front that read "Good laundry work done here." This image gives little indication that the area flourished with several mills and small industries.

Titicus had a flourishing general store (right), which over the years sold a wide range of goods, from feed and grain to penny candy. An early proprietor was John Dempster Nash, who in 1885 was appointed postmaster of Titicus District. He lived next door at 2 Mapleshade Road (left), which stands today as a well-maintained home. The store is used as a residence, and by Wildlife Artists.

By 1761 the Titicus district had its own school where all grades were taught in one room. This remained the case until the end of the 19th century, when a wing was added to the rear. The 1909 building, shown here, served as a school until 1939, and now serves as the American Legion headquarters, and is used on Sundays by the Assembly of God.

The machine shop at North Salem Road and New Street was run by Orville Sprague (seated). As he had shortened and paralyzed legs he moved on a wheeled board among his machines, which were set close to the floor. He reached his living-quarters below by sliding down a pole. With him is William Casey. To the left is "Old Muck." The building, 61 North Salem Road, is now a home.

The Bellagamba family lived in Titicus in the home that is now 8 North Street. In the center with the accordion is Alessandro (Henry) Bellagamba. His wife, Franchina, stands behind him to his right. Others in the group are family members and boarders (who paid $3 a month rent and helped buy the food), as the usual number at the daily dinner table was 19.

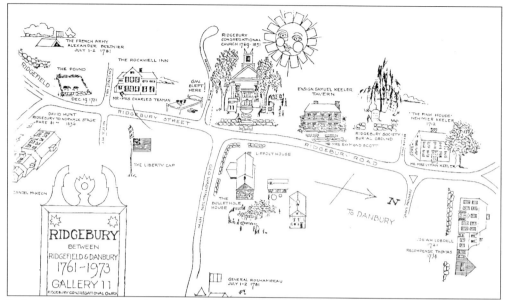

Before the American Revolution, northwestern Ridgefield was a populous hamlet with taverns, stores, two churches, and some modest industry. In April 1777, British troops marched through Ridgebury after they burned Danbury. Four years later, General Rochambeau and his French army camped in fields along Ridgebury Road en route to Yorktown. This sketch marked a 1973 event at the church.

Ridgebury had two school districts in the 1800s. By 1928, when this picture was taken, enrollment had dwindled to ten students. By the following year the school was closed and the children transferred to another school. The building at Ridgebury and Stagecoach Roads was moved across the street and made into a home owned by Daniel M. McKeon. Today it is still recognizable as a former schoolhouse.

50

At the intersection of Shadow Lake and Ridgebury Roads stands the Pink House, one of the town's oldest buildings. This early saltbox is virtually unchanged and has remained in the family of Capt. Nehemiah Keeler. The old homestead has been painted pink for as long as anyone can remember, but the trees and fence are long gone.

Pictured here is a picnic at the Pink House on July 4, *c.* 1910. Three Keeler women prepare a spread at the family farm. The large barn and fields were across the road.

Capt. Henry Whitney's house is at the intersection of Old Stagecoach and Ridgebury Roads. Whitney's son-in-law, David Hunt, established a stage line from Ridgebury to Norwalk, and the house became a stop when the stagecoach line extended northward. Daniel M. McKeon purchased the home in 1939. He and his late wife, Louise, played an important role in the political, historical, and cultural life of the town.

Mr. And Mrs. Samuel A. Coe are shown here on the porch of the Whitney house, which was their home from the late 1880s until the 1930s. Sam Coe, who lost his arm in the Civil War, served as selectman, assessor, and deacon of the Ridgebury Congregational Church. He was recognized as the unofficial mayor of the town's northwestern section.

The southeastern section of Ridgefield has been called Branchville since the early part of the 19th century. Shown here in the 1920s, Branchville was a thriving little village with stores, mills, a hotel, a machinery factory, a noted mineral quarry, a post office, and a school. In the early part of the 20th century a large number of Italians arrived and found work in the area, turning it into an Italian enclave. On the far right in this old postcard is the Ancona family's first market, now larger and in a new location on the hill behind this property. The Branchville railroad station was constructed in the mid-1850s when the Danbury-Norwalk line opened. Today it is part of Metro North, and is used heavily by commuters on their way to work in Stamford and New York City.

The Branchville Fresh Air Association was organized in 1899, and for many years thousands of New York City youngsters were brought here for several weeks in the summer to be given a taste of country life.

The Branchville General Store, owned by the DeBenigno family, is shown here in the 1920s. The store was the center of the Italian community in both the Branchville and Georgetown areas. Newly arrived immigrants were welcomed and frequently housed there until they found work and homes of their own. Today the building is the home of the Soho Gallery, and is on the National Historic Register.

Branchville residents identified strongly with their neighborhood. Members of the Branchville Civic Association are shown here clearing ground to build the playground that gave its name to Playground Road. Joe Ancona Jr. and Sr., Ray Platt, Frank D'Addario, Rick Rudolph, and his son Gene are loading a 1930–31 Chevy truck.

The flood of 1955, which was caused by days of heavy rainfall, wreaked havoc in many Connecticut towns. Ridgefield was spared for the most part, but many streams and rivers overflowed their banks. Along the Norwalk River, the low-lying area of Branchville was under water, including the railroad tracks. This scene was photographed just west of the railroad station.

Children are sledding and playing in the snow on Catoonah Street after a blizzard in 1934. Officially laid out in 1721, it was originally called Burt's Lane after Benjamin Burt, the town's first blacksmith, and later renamed New West Lane. In 1867 the name was again changed, this time to Catoonah after Chief Catoonah, the sachem of the Ramapoo Indians who sold land to the town's first settlers.

David F. Bedient, longtime Catoonah Street resident and general store proprietor, sits atop the Ann Smith house with his own home directly behind him. The small annex to the Smith house served as a post office. The house later became the Old Paint Shop; following that, it was attractively renovated and now serves as a law office at 36 Catoonah Street.

In 1889 M.B. Whitlock's livery stable advertised: "careful drivers always furnished." Shown here around 1912, it later became Sperry's Stable. It was one of several commercial enterprises at the eastern end of the street, including hat, shirt, and candlestick factories. Along with boarding and grooming horses for the community, it provided the horses needed to draw equipment for the fire department across the street.

On January 17, 1948, after days of heavy snow and freezing weather, during which many eyes watched rafters separate from supports, the roof of the grand old building collapsed. In its many uses it had seen the horse give way to the automobile, coal give way to oil, and the activities of war replace those of peace.

The new fire department was built in 1908 after spending its first few years in the basement of the town hall, which had been rebuilt after the Great Fire of 1895. The destruction of the downtown area brought home the urgency of making many village improvements, including the creation of a fire department. It was staffed entirely by volunteers until the 1930s, when the first paid fireman was appointed. Throughout the years, several additions have been made to the original building.

Peter McGlynn owned a Rambler, one of the earliest cars in town. This 1908 photograph shows two of his five children—three-year-old Helen and six-year-old Joe—with their aunt, Jane Hennelly. The family lived at 31 Catoonah Street. When Helen married Don "Stub" Cumming, she moved across the street to No. 28, where she was still living at the age of 94 when this book went to print in 1999.

A school, homes, businesses, and stores have long been intermingled on Bailey Avenue, a little street at the heart of the village. Many oldtimers will remember Coleman's Lunch Wagon, a former railroad coach that held no more than 20 people at one time. It was replaced by Herb Bates livery service and later by the Acorn Press. Charles Crouchley's plumbing shop and Charles Reidinger's electrical business were across the street.

Farther down Bailey Avenue children are shown lined up outside the Center School. It was the town's largest grammar school until the new one opened up on East Ridge in 1915. The building served as the high school until 1927, when it lost its bleak look and became the Garden School, housing kindergarten and first grade students. It was torn down in the 1950s and was replaced by a parking lot.

The Brunetti & Gasperini General Store was on the corner of Bailey Avenue and Prospect Street. It carried meats and groceries, yard goods, shoes, and some kitchen utensils. Hugh Montanari is seated on the sacks, and next to him is the young man who delivered groceries, which were usually ordered by phone.

Inside the store are the two proprietors, Ernesto Brunetti (left) and Nazzareno Gasperini (right). Gasperini started the store while he was still foreman at the Port of Missing Men. "Tabby" Carboni (center) was the bookkeeper. The store specialized in the traditional foods of the growing Italian population. "When winter work was scarce, my father carried accounts for several months," says Mary Gasperini Paterniani.

The Italian American Citizens Political Club was formed on June 29, 1913. As membership in the club grew, a larger meeting place was needed, so land was purchased on Prospect Street, up the street a little from Brunetti and Gasperini's market. By 1915 the members voted to change their name and the club evolved into a mutual aid society that has continued to play a key role in the life of the town's Italian American community.

Members of the Italian American Club enjoy their annual banquet at the hall in the late 1920s. On this occasion, Dick Venus (front row, left) and his band had been invited to perform. The club is still a popular place for meetings and celebrations, one such being a festival on the grounds that features the traditional roasting of the "porchetta."

The Florida District School was among the five earliest schools maintained by the town. This undated photograph shows its location at the junction of Florida and Florida Hill Roads. Ridgefield was an agricultural community and the land was cleared for fields and pastures.

Downsbury Manor was the home of Col. Edward Knox, a hat manufacturer and Civil War hero. His 45-room house, on 300 acres at the top of Florida Hill Road, had an indoor riding ring, elaborate gardens, and a commanding view of the surrounding hills. Mark Twain came by train from his home in Redding to visit his friend. After the death of Colonel Knox, the house changed hands several times until it was torn down and the land subdivided.

George Washington Gilbert was born in 1847, and for unknown reasons he lived the life of a hermit for over 40 years. He received many visitors whom he entertained with stories and riddles. He lived near the Knox estate, and when his ancestral home collapsed around him, Colonel Knox furnished him with a new, cozy house. He was found dead in his home in 1925, and is buried in the Florida Cemetery on Route 7.

The Hermit and Hermitage, George Washington Gilbert, Ridgefield, Conn.

West Mountain is the site of Round Pond, the town's largest body of natural water (32 acres) and its highest. In early days the pond provided power for a sawmill and a place to fish. Later it was a source of ice for refrigeration, and has long been used for town water. It was also a perfect place for skating and sledding.

Sleigh rides on West Mountain were both enjoyable and a useful means of winter travel. David Dougherty Sr. is shown here driving Mr. and Mrs. John Hampton Lynch in a Russian sleigh.

Five
BEYOND THE VILLAGE

In 1810, master carpenter Albin Jennings built a home for his new bride on what is now Danbury Road, on the site of the Fox Hill Condominiums. The property was purchased by Col. Louis D. Conley, who owned 2,000 acres in the Bennett's Farm area. The old home was remodeled and enlarged, and opened in the 1920s as a restaurant called the Outpost Inn, named after his famed Outpost Nursery. Colonel Conley drained the swampy area in front of the house and built Outpost Pond, a favorite ice skating spot for many years. The restaurant, which was popular even through the Depression years, was a favorite spot for weddings, luncheons, dances, and political and business meetings. There are still many noted restaurants in Ridgefield, but in its time the Outpost Inn was one of the best.

"Hickories" was the Lounsbury family homestead in the Farmingville area. George Lounsbury (inset) was a teacher and minister of the Episcopal Church until poor health led him to leave the ministry. In 1894 he entered politics and served as state senator from 1895 to 1899, and as governor from 1899 to 1901. He became president of the First National Bank. Hickories is now the Brewster property on Lounbury Road.

While still governor, Mr. Lounsbury presented a new Farmingville School to the town on land that had been donated by the Starr family. George Rockwell, a town historian and nephew of George Lounsbury, is standing to the right of the building. The third school to be built on that site was constructed in the 1960s.

David L. Jones is shown with his team of oxen at the gates to Walnut Grove Farm in Farmingville, where he settled in 1890. The late Karl Nash, publisher of the *Ridgefield Press*, spent his childhood summers at this farm, which belonged to his grandparents.

Marie Kendall took this view of a dairy herd on Walnut Grove Farm at the turn of the century. Farmingville Road is in the background, lined with stone walls. In 1964 the land was purchased and subdivided, and homes were built on 48 of the 96 acres.

Mamanasco Lake, or Mamanasquag as it was called in the early days, means "grassy pond." It has been the center of year-round activity for over 300 years. Shown here is the Dixon family gathered on the boathouse dock. The estate known as "Nydeggen" can be seen in the distance.

In winter the lake was a favorite spot for ice skating; summer activities included picnicking, fishing, swimming, and canoeing. Gaetano (Henry) Giardini enjoys a day's outing at Lake Mamanasco with the Andrew Mei family in 1914.

A young Ferdinand Bedini poses in the middle of his award-winning vegetable garden at the Vincent Bedini family home on North Salem Road. Mr. Bedini still loves to garden, albeit on a much smaller scale. Today Mr. and Mrs. David Erich own the home.

Leon Sauve was the farm manager on the estate of Miss Anne S. Richardson on North Salem Road. Upon her death, Miss Richardson left her land to the town with instructions that her home was to be taken down. The farmhouse and part of the farm is now the home of Aldo and Gloria Biagiotti.

Farmers and merchants continued to use horse-drawn wagons for many years after trucks and automobiles appeared in Ridgefield. Will Beers, a relative of the William Francis Casey family, is shown here transporting some of his farm produce.

In 1928, Irving B. Conklin established Conklin's Dairy, which served the community for many years. Employees of the dairy are seen in front of a Conklin's delivery truck on the farm on Ramapoo Road.

In April 1905, as the 8:20 a.m. train out of Ridgefield Station was rounding a curve at the Ivy Hill power station, the engine and coal tender broke loose. They were at the head of the train and running backward to ease the train down the hill when they became disconnected. The engine rammed the tender and they jumped the track, turned on their sides, and dug into the hillside. The engineer, William Horan, was pinned under the cab and scalded to death by the escaping steam. Passengers and other crewmembers escaped with minor injuries. In 1925 passenger service on this branch was discontinued.

A quiet country scene, this is Nod Road looking south before it was paved. The farm, owned by Mrs. Priscilla (Chisolm) Lee, was managed by Vincenzo Tulipani.

The five Tulipani boys are seen after a morning of "hilling potatoes." There was a parade in town, but chores came first, and one of the brothers reported that they had to miss the parade.

Little Aldo Biagiotti and his mother, Giovanna Biagiotti, are seated in a friend's car in front of their home. The house on Danbury Road was said to have a ghost, although it never seemed to bother the family.

The Giardini and Mei families are ready to visit friends at the Port of Missing Men, just over the line in New York. After settling in Ridgefield, they returned to their old quarters on Sunday afternoons for picnics, games, and music.

The Port of Missing Men was a restaurant and teahouse. It was built at the turn of the century by Henry B. Anderson on 1,750 acres on the crest of a ridge on Titicus Mountain. One third of the property was in Connecticut—the rest was in New York State. The place was famous for its sweeping views of the surrounding hills and valleys.

H.B. Anderson was instrumental in bringing many Italian workers to Ridgefield, first to build the sewer and water systems, then to build the roads on the Port of Missing Men acreage, where he hoped to develop an upscale residential community. Mr. Anderson is shown seated in the back of his handsome carriage.

Young women from Ridgefield were employed at the Port of Missing Men as waitresses in the teahouse. Second from the right is Yole Casagrande, who at 13 began working there during the summers. She still lives in Ridgefield, as does Rica Manna, second from the left.

Frank Marcucci and his wife, Mary, managed the resort in its last years. Below the stairs was a room where coachmen and chauffeurs ate, having driven their employers to the popular restaurant on the mountain. Frank is proudly holding supper—a pheasant he apparently shot.

The farm of American impressionist Julien Alden Weir straddles the Ridgefield-Wilton border, and is Connecticut's only National Historic Site. This view of the buildings from the north shows sculptor Mahonri Young, Weir's son-in-law. His studio was the building on the far right. (Weir Farm Archives.)

In 1897 J. Alden Weir and Childe Hassam founded the influential Ten American Painters (pictured above). Their works are among the finest of American Impressionism. They are, from left to right, as follows: (seated) Edward Simmons, Willard Metcalf, Childe Hassam, J. Alden Weir, and Robert Reid; (standing) William M. Chase, Frank Benson, Edmund Tarbell, Thomas Dewing, and Joseph Decamp. (Weir Farm Archives.)

Mr. Weir loved fishing and outdoor sports. He built his own pond to ensure a plentiful supply of fish. Today a walk around the pond is an enjoyable part of a visit to the historic site. (Weir Farm Archives.)

This fishing bridge near Weir Pond was the subject of a 1915 painting called *The Fishing Party*. The farm inspired subject matter for Weir and his friends Childe Hassam, John Twachtman, and Albert Pinkham Ryder. (Weir Farm Archives.)

Ridgefielders often spent vacations at nearby lakes. The Willis Gilberts had a cottage at Lake Waccabuc before it became a private area. The huge granite rock at the edge of the lake was called "The Ovens."

A young Gilbert relative, Willis Boyce, enjoys a canoe ride on Lake Waccabuc with his dog Trixie.

Six

VISITORS WHO
CAME AND STAYED

In the late 1800s Ridgefield's natural beauty and the railroad accounted for the towns rise as a summer resort. Equally important, however, was the enterprising spirit of J. Howard King, who opened High Ridge to the real estate market. What had been common country fields were now lined with grand homes (including the Doubleday Mansion, shown here), and the area became one of the most delightful spots to spend the summer months. Country seats were built close around the village and in the outlying regions.

"Graeloe" was the Main Street estate developed in 1887 by Lucius Horatio Biglow. The home of Revolutionary War hero Col. Philip Burr Bradley was incorporated into a much larger house and moved back from the road. Mr. Biglow, a New York music publisher, combined his wife's maiden name, Graham, and his own to give the estate its name, still to be seen on a pillar at the entrance.

Mrs. Lucius Biglow (seated, center) is pictured on the porch at Graeloe with, from left to right, her granddaughter Anne, her daughter, Elizabeth Ballard, her granddaughter Elizabeth, and her grandson Edward. In 1964 Mrs. Ballard left her property to the town for a park, with the provision that the house be torn down. Ballard Park has beautiful trees, a flower garden, a bandstand, and a children's playground.

In 1893, George M. Olcott built his Italianate mansion "Casagmo" on the site of the old Stebbins house on north Main Street. The name combined Casa (Italian for house) and the initials of its builder, G.M.O. This grand house was torn down in the late 1960s for the town's first large-scale apartment development. Some of the estate's grandeur can be seen in the remaining stone walls of its terraced gardens.

Miss Mary L.B. Olcott was the mistress of Casagmo after the death of her father. She was a published poet and wrote the lines memorializing the Battle of Ridgefield. An ardent feminist, she was active in the woman's suffrage movement, and in her later years devoted herself to genealogy, gardening, and the breeding of prize poodles, game birds, and swans at Casagmo.

Hawks Nest was the 40-room, 30-acre estate of Mr. and Mrs. W.S. Hawk at the intersection of Branchville and East Ridge Roads, near the present-day middle school. The mansion was built in the late 1890s at a cost of $40,000. Although summer residents, Mr. and Mrs. Hawk were generous, community-minded citizens and helped finance the rebuilding of the town hall after it was destroyed by fire. They also donated money to build the sidewalk around the new Ridgefield Library.

Unfortunately, the Hawks did not have long to enjoy their new home. In newly discovered photographs, the Phineas C. Lounsbury Engine Company is seen fighting the blaze that destroyed the elegant mansion. Esther Nash Kelly, a student at the "old" high school on East Ridge, recalls being allowed to watch the blaze from her classroom window. Only the gates to the estate and the carriagehouse remain standing today.

WICKOPEE FARM.   RIDGEFIELD, CONN.
HOME OF B. OGDEN CHISHOLM.

Wickopee Farm was the home of B. Ogden Chisolm, who purchased land on Peaceable Street in 1902. He was secretary-treasurer of the Greenwich Savings Bank in New York City, an international inspector of prisons, and a prolific writer on his travels and findings. B.O., as he preferred to be called, was much involved in affairs of the town.

Mr. and Mrs. Chisolm are shown in the center of this photo with four of their seven daughters. From the left to right are Elizabeth, Winifred Chisolm Brown, Margaret, and Priscilla. Son-in-law Curtis Brown is at the far right. Mrs. Chisolm holds Lupo, a Pekingnese. Another Pekingnese and a German Shepherd puppy are included in the family photo. Priscilla Chisolm Lee's daughter, Mrs. David Watson, lives in Ridgefield.

Ready for a parade, the seven costumed Chisolm daughters are shown above with their goat cart ambulance "just in case of an accident." The home of farm superintendent Julius Tulipani, seen in the background, and the barn next to it were torn down in the early 1990s to make way for a new subdivision. Below, a farm worker is seen cutting hay in the field as fodder for the farm animals.

B.O. Chisolm prepares to take a twirl on the ice with his youngest daughter, Priscilla. As New York businessmen retired, the "summer people" became year-round residents. This was encouraged by Editor White of the *Ridgefield Press*, who wrote in 1902, "we only need confidence and a certain amount of push and enterprise, and half the summer houses in Ridgefield will be winter homes as well."

Chisolm family members go out by sled to cut down their Christmas tree.

The photograph above shows the home of Mr. and Mrs. John H. Lynch under construction on West Mountain, c. 1910. There were various outbuildings, gardens, tennis courts, and a swimming pool on the grounds. The house enjoyed a spectacular view of the three lakes (Waccabuc, Rippowam and Oscaleta) and toward the Hudson River and the mountains to the west. In 1962 the property was sold to the Congregation of Notre Dame, who use the facility as a motherhouse. The Landmark Academy now uses the school built on the property by the congregation.

The Lynch family is seen here at the front entrance of their West Mountain farm residence. From left to right are John Hampton Lynch Jr.; his father, John Hampton Lynch Sr.; Madeleine Lynch Emerson; sons Russell (front), Hampton(the eldest), and Simpson; and Mrs. John Lynch Sr. (Lucy Moffitt Lynch).

David Dougherty Sr. is sitting on a horse-drawn thresher, cutting hay on the Lynch Farm. Hampton Lynch and his father are watching in the center, and to the left are friends who visited and enjoyed seeing farm work. The farm produced vegetables, fruit, eggs, milk, and meat for the family, their workers, and their tenants.

Ontaroga Farm, the family home of Mr. and Mrs. Louis Morris Starr, is on Farmingville Road, where it meets Lounsbury Road. Traditionally painted yellow, the house with its gracious porch still stands.

Mrs. Louis Morris Starr poses at Ontaroga Farm in 1899 with one of her three daughters, Caroline Margaret, who would later be Mrs. Theodore C. Jessup. The Lynch and Starr families were linked when the Lynch's son John married Emeline, one of the three Starr daughters. Their daughter, Mrs. Joseph Wittman, lives in Ridgefield.

"Homewood," the estate built by George Griswold Haven on West Lane, had extensive acreage and many outbuildings, including stables for the horses that were his passion. This interest, shared by others in town, sometimes turned Main Street into a raceway on Sunday afternoons, when teams owned by Dr. Van Saun, Edward Dutton, William Keeler, and George Haven were cheered to the finish line. Mr. Haven was usually the winner. The photograph below shows him out for a drive, coachman behind—an enjoyable sight for Ridgefielders.

Rufus H. King, whose family in Ridgefield dates back to the Revolution, built this elegant Victorian mansion in the early 1870s. The house stood on the southwest corner of High Ridge and Peaceable Street, but caught fire around 1903 and burned to the ground. Mr. King moved his family across the intersection to the white house at the northeast corner of High Ridge and King Lane, where he died a year later. Visible on the side porch are members of the family ready for a bicycle ride.

Frederic E. Lewis, a jovial and witty man, named his showcase estate on West Lane "Upagenstit" (Up Against It). Specimen trees and shrubs, abundant flowers, and prize orchids were grown on the grounds and in his greenhouses. The mansion had an indoor, Olympic-sized, glass-domed swimming pool.

Each week during the winter months, Fred Minnerly drove the estate's truck to New York City, loaded with wood for the 52nd Street home of Mr. and Mrs. Lewis. There were regular trips, too, with flowers, meat, vegetables, milk, and butter. The Lewises provided many services and benefits for the community, and their son established the Wadsworth Lewis Fund, which today supports many local organizations.

Bob Maxwell, one of three chauffeurs employed by F.E. Lewis, is pictured sitting at the wheel of a 1919 Packard, in front of the entrance to Upagenstit. The stone pillars still stand and mark the entrance to the estate subdivision at Manor Road and West Lane.

The Ridgefield Chauffeurs Ball of 1912 took place at the town hall. In the early 1900s cars replaced carriages, and coachmen became chauffeurs. As their numbers grew they formed an association and each year held a ball, a gala full-dress event, that continued through the 1930s, until owners began driving their own cars and World War II dawned.

Seven

LEARNING AND PLAYING

"We are on our way to the new school" is how the sign reads as children parade up Main Street in the Old Home Day and Fourth of July celebration in 1914. The event was to celebrate the laying of the cornerstone for the new Benjamin Franklin Grammar School that was to be built on East Ridge. The parade to the new school started at 10:30 in the morning, and was followed by children's games, exercises, a maypole dance, a baseball game, and a band concert. The celebration was topped off by fireworks and a torch illumination.

The town appropriated the sum of $40,000 in 1913 to build a new grammar school. Shown here in a rare photograph loaned by Walter Boyce, is the school under construction.

World War I had begun, and schoolchildren are shown here doing their part for the war effort by tending their victory gardens at the Benjamin Franklin School. The little girl with hoes over her shoulder is Mary Creagh. She would one day become a teacher.

This Hartmann photograph of the graduating Ridgefield High School Class of 1925 shows two of the fourteen graduates who went on to become teachers in the Ridgefield school system. Mary Creagh, who still lives on North Street, is shown seated on the far right, and Elsa Hartmann, who was the daughter of the photographer, Joseph Hartmann, is standing in the back row.

Mabel Cleves arrived in Ridgefield in 1898, "fired with enthusiasm for the new great educational philosophy of Dr. Maria Montessori." She is shown here in the back row on the left, with a kindergarten class in the early 1920s. Miss Cleves, who retired in 1938, was one of the founders of Ridgefield's modern school system.

The Vinton School on East Ridge was a boarding school for girls run by sisters Elizabeth and Gertrude Vinton. The school, which graduated young ladies ready to enter the world of education and social work, moved to Pomfret, Connecticut, in 1905.

GRAY COURT COLLEGE, RIDGEFIELD, CONNECTICUT

Gray Court College, a junior college, was established in 1941 in what had long been known as Upagenstit, the massive mansion and estate of Frederic E. Lewis. The school's motto, Esto perpetua (which means "it is perpetual"), proved far from true as the fledgling institution closed its doors just after World War II.

In 1907 Dr. Roland J. Mulford established the Ridgefield School for Boys on Main Street. The buildings were used during the school term as a boarding school, and in the summer months were used as an inn. In 1911 the school moved to a new campus on 115 acres, on the eastern side of Titicus Mountain off North Salem Road. The building was four stories high and had 100 rooms. In 1922 Theodore Jessup succeeded Dr. Mulford as headmaster. The school closed in 1938, but some of the property remains in private hands.

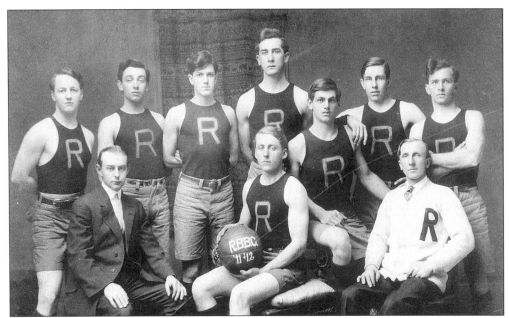

The game of basketball came to Ridgefield in 1908. The new team played against Danbury in their first game, losing 21-7. Meanwhile, in a building behind St. Stephen's Church, another team was practicing. It was the St. Stephen's Athletic Association, led by Francis Martin. St. Stephen's challenged the Ridgefield team to three games, winning two out of three. It wasn't long before the two teams combined and played as one.

Some sports in Ridgefield have flourished briefly and died. Others have survived, but baseball has always remained the number one sport. Only a few played the game back in the old days, but today hundreds of boys and girls are part of Little League and girls' softball. Charles Crouchly Sr., shown here holding his son Ralph, organized the first baseball team before the turn of the 20th century. Clifford Holleran is shown below with the 1926–27 Hamilton High baseball team. Coach Holleran came to Ridgefield in 1920 as principal of the high school and as a math and science teacher. He began immediately organizing the baseball and basketball teams. His tenure as coach of both teams lasted for 20 years. Upon retirement from teaching, "Kip" Holleran became director of the Boys' Club, a position he held for 14 years.

The first women's sports team to appear in Ridgefield was the Catoonah Street Basketball Club, which was coached by Francis Martin. Shown here in 1901, the teams played until the outbreak of World War I.

There have been many winning baseball teams throughout the years. By the 1930s the high school teams were so good that they began to play with the larger schools in the area, and the 1940 team went on to the state semi-finals. In 1946 they were the Class B Fairfield County champs.

Eight

A MUSICAL TOWN

Music has always been an important part of life in Ridgefield. Patriotic celebrations, parades, concerts, musicals, minstrel shows, and more provided townspeople with entertainment before the advent of movies and television. The first Ridgefield Band was organized in 1838 with about 20 members. In 1861 seven members of the band joined the army and served as musicians during the Civil War. In 1901 it became the Oreneca Band and continued through the World War I era. As the town grew, many musical groups began to appear. Back then, as now, big band, swing, and country and western were the rage, and Ridgefield had music groups to play it all. Besides restaurants and dance halls in the area, these bands performed regularly at the Odd Fellows Hall (located on Main Street then), in the town hall, and on local radio stations.

Ridgefield's Music Man, Aldo Casagrande, who had been playing cornet with the old Oreneca Band since 1904, organized the Ridgefield Boys' Band in 1926. Seen here is the fledgling band in their first uniforms, navy blue sweaters with red trim and white duck pants. Navy blue caps with red trim completed the outfit. They marched in their first Memorial Day parade in 1927.

By 1934, when this photograph was taken in front of the town hall, the name of the band had been changed to Oreneca. The boys, looking smart in their new green uniforms, are about to march in the Memorial Day parade. Band Master Casagrande is holding his cornet and is standing behind the drum.

The Ridgefield High School Class of 1932 performed *Washington's Operetta* in December, 1931, in preparation for the upcoming town-wide celebration to celebrate the birth of George Washington 200 years earlier.

The class play of 1947 was *Patton's Muscle B Ranch*, directed by Eleanor Burdick. Miss Burdick, who taught American and European history, as well as English, spent many years directing the high school plays that were presented on the town hall stage.

The Ridgefield Men's Quartet sang on radio station WICC in Bridgeport weekly for several years. Shown here from left to right are Willis Boyce, Llewellyn Crossman, Charles Wade Walker, and Albert Baynham.

Charlotte (Lottie) Boyce was a concert pianist who performed throughout the area, and was the organist at St. Stephen's Church. In this Hartmann photograph Mrs. Boyce is shown at the piano in her home, where for many years she gave piano lessons. She and her husband, Willis, were also popular musicians with the dance bands at Odd Fellows Hall.

The Mayflower Swing Band is shown here as it played for the 1938 Chauffeurs' Ball in the town hall. Richard Venus, town historian, frequently led the band, but in this photograph he is the happy drummer in the back row. In earlier years Dick played in the Ridgefield Boys' Band, then with the Oreneca Band.

The Sagebrush Serenaders are seen playing at the Congregational Church House back in the 1940s. The caller and singer was George Thompson; Bud Morrisroe played fiddle; Albert Tulipani played guitar; Alfred Tulipani played bass; Aldo Tulipani played accordion; and Albert Ahlgum played banjo. The Tulipani group became a popular fixture on Saturday night at the Odd Fellows Hall.

Al's Old Timers was another dance band that was popular with the square dance crowd at the Odd Fellows Hall. From left to right are Lou Girolmetti, Walter Boyce, Don McGuire, Al Broadhurst, Frank Lancaster, Lew Gay, Allan Sterry, and Willis Boyce.

This high school band is practicing for a performance in the mid-1940s. Faces that might be recognized are as follows, from left to right: Bud Morrisroe, banjo; Walter Boyce, bass; Vivien Hull, piano; Lou Girolmetti, accordion; Ed Burn, trumpet; John Franzmann, violin; and Frank Lancaster, drums.

Nine

JOSEPH HARTMANN: IMAGES OF RIDGEFIELD

Joseph Hartmann was born in 1867 in Pffafenhofen, Germany, one of six children in a doctor's family. In Muran, Austria (now Murano, Italy), he served as an apprentice photographer. In 1888, when he was 21, he emigrated to the U.S. and obtained employment with Havee, a postcard company in Stamford, Connecticut. He opened a photography studio on the third floor of the Bedient Building on Main Street, and in 1898 he married Amalie L. Diedrich (1867–1943), who had been working as a German teacher for the children of the Rufus King family on High Ridge. Joseph and Amalie had three children, Werner, Erhard, and Elsa.

Joseph Hartmann operated his studio until his retirement in 1938. He died in 1943, leaving a legacy of many thousands of glass-plate negatives, now a part of the archives of the Keeler Tavern Museum. Through his superb photographic collection he recreated life in Ridgefield during the early 20th century.

A group of lifelong Ridgefielders met once a week for several years at the Keeler Tavern Museum, helping to identify the subjects in thousands of Hartmann glass plates. Each image was projected onto a TV screen, and through an attached VCR was transformed from a negative to a positive image. Not only were the museum historians able to catalog the vast collection, but names were given to many of the previously unidentified subjects, and a valuable oral history was recorded as well. The subject to the left remains unidentified, but the gentleman below on the left is Joseph Ancona, who came from Sicily in the early years of the 20th century. After serving in France during World War I, he returned to Ridgefield, where he opened a grocery store in the Branchville area of town. Nearly 75 years have passed since then; the business has grown, but both the market and wine shop are still owned by the Ancona family. The gentleman below on the right is Allesandro (Henry) Bellagamba, who came to this country from the Ancona region in Italy.

Ethel Martin Walters and John Walters were members of the Mandolin Club, a popular group during the 1920s. In 1926 they appeared on the first broadcast of WICC radio in Bridgeport, Connecticut.

One night's hunt on October 25, 1904, is recreated in the studio of Joseph Hartmann. From left to right are Will Roth, Sam Seymour, Mally Knapp, and Charles Stevens.

Doris Godfrey Martin and Francis Martin were married for over 50 years. Doris was known for her involvement in the activities of the Methodist Church and her beautiful singing voice. Marty was "Mr. Ridgefield," involving himself in many church and civic activities. His generosity, both with time and money, enriched the lives of all in the community. Doris and Marty loved to dance, and held parties at the barn on their North Salem Road property, and ice skating parties in the winter on Lake Mamanasco.

Sisters Katherine and Mary O'Hearn pose with their cousin, Molly Rainey. The O'Hearn girls taught school locally for many years.

William O. Seymour is shown here with his grandson, Karl Seymour Nash. William ran a school for boys in the old Goodrich home, now the Peter Parley house on High Ridge. He was the railroad commissioner for the state of Connecticut and a delegate to the Constitutional Convention in 1902, as well as being active in the Masons and serving as the chairman of the 1908 bicentennial celebration. Karl was the owner of the *Ridgefield Press* for over 50 years.

The Bedini family is pictured enjoying a day's outing *c.* 1915. They are, from left to right, Alexander, David, Cesira, her son Ferdinand, Joseph, Vincenzo (Cesira's husband), and Frank.

Mourning the death of his wife, Philomena, Antonio Gaeta is seen wearing a black arm band. The children are James, Tony, and Domenick. Their only daughter, Rose, is not pictured.

Mr. and Mrs. Achille Bacchiochi pose with their four sons: James (front), Aldo, Joseph, and Don. Mr. Achille owned a successful construction company that, upon his retirement, was taken over by his sons.

Mr. and Mrs. Daniel J. Tobin pose with their son Daniel, who became a local builder and was one of the many Tobins to live on Silver Spring Road.

The Gilbert name is an old one in the history of Ridgefield. Mr. and Mrs. Willis Gilbert are shown here with their daughters, Eleanora and Abby. Mr. Gilbert owned a shoe store on Main Street. Along with being politically active in town, he served as postmaster from 1916 to 1924.

Nazzareno Torcellini and his wife, Matilda (Paterniani) Torcellini, are shown here with their daughter Elsie. The Torcellinis had two other daughters, Ann and Louise, all of whom still live in Ridgefield.

Although these two little girls remain unidentified, their beauty and innocence has been captured forever. It was Ridgefield's fortune when Joseph Hartmann decided to set up his photography studio on Main Street, where he photographed the faces of its people for almost 50 years.

114

Mario and Maria Girolmetti (left) stood up for newlyweds Domenico and Ida (Montanari) Fossi at their wedding in 1923. The Fossis were very active in the Italian Club, where Domenico would stay up all night cooking the porchetta for Field Day. They had seven children, one of whom, Louis, served as first selectman for eight years.

Mr. and Mrs. Mortimer Keeler are shown here with their family. Descended from the early Keeler settlers, Mortimer and his family lived on their farm in the Whipstick district. Mrs. Keeler was a member of the Ridgefield branch of the National League of Women Voters, which was organized in 1921. They were both charter members of Grange No. 165, Patrons of Husbandry, which was organized in Ridgefield in 1906.

Mrs. Vincent Bedini poses with her sons, Ferdinand and Silvio. Ferdinand remained in Ridgefield, carrying on the family business, and has been active in community affairs throughout his life. Silvio went on to become a curator at the Smithsonian Institution in Washington, D.C. One of the many books he authored, *Ridgefield in Review*, was written for the 250th anniversary of the town's founding.

Having worked throughout Europe as a stonemason, Ettore Frattini arrived in the U.S. in 1901. He is shown here with his wife, Antonia, and their four daughters.

Above Left: Kathyrn Venus, now Mrs. Paul Rosa, is a founder of the Keeler Tavern Museum, and longtime chairman of the Ridgefield Historic District. She and her husband have been involved in many local historical and civic groups.

Above Right: Helen and Catherine Tobin are the daughters of Mr. and Mrs. Daniel Tobin. The girls attended the West Lane schoolhouse and as young women entered the teaching profession.

Right: Jack Cranston and his half-sister, Alice Mullen, portray the sweetness of youth in an early Hartmann photograph.

Mary and Richard Venus were two of the nine children born to Charles and Mary Elizabeth Fahey Venus. This sweet little boy grew into manhood to become one of Ridgefield's greatest treasures. He started working at age seven with a newspaper route, and retired from the post office after serving for 21 years as postmaster. In addition to his many careers, Dick has managed to be an actor and musician, a politician, a writer and storyteller, the town historian, and the devoted husband of Marie, to whom he has been married since 1940.

Mary and Margaret Ryan are two of the three Ryan daughters, the children of Will and Ethel McGlynn Ryan. Will Ryan was the Ryan of the McGlynn and Ryan Plumbing business on Main Street.

118

Ten

THE 1930s, 1940s, AND 1950s

"Kit" and "Lady," Richard Venus's percheron mares, are waiting their turn to join the tercentenary parade on July 4, 1935. It was the 300th anniversary of the founding of the state of Connecticut, and Ridgefielders joined in with great enthusiasm. These were the Depression years and times were not easy in Ridgefield, but spirits remained high. Many families had vegetable gardens and fruit orchards, they hunted for meat and game, made their own clothes, and baked, canned, and provided for themselves and their neighbors. For amusement there were parades and celebrations, Grange activities, the Danbury Fair, plays, dances, movies, and sports. Then the war came, and, as in communities across the America, townspeople began working together for a common cause. In the post-war years the village of Ridgefield began to grow. Word spread of Ridgefield's natural beauty, its good schools, and a fairly easy commute to New York City, and so the next wave of people started coming. This book takes the reader through the end of the 1950s, just before the population explosion and building boom began.

Patriotism was at its highest on Memorial Day, 1942, as the nation was at war. The proud marchers in the foreground are, from left to right, Grand Marshall Harry E. Hull, Anne Richardson, and Julius Tulipani. Anne Richardson was a longtime chairman of the Village Improvement Committee of the Ridgefield Garden Club. Richardson Park and the high school property on North Salem Road were part of her property.

Geraldine Farrar was a world-renowned opera singer who came to live in Ridgefield when she retired from the Metropolitan Opera in 1931. During the war she joined both the Red Cross and the American Women's Volunteer Services. Shown here at a war bond rally in 1943, she is holding a pig to be auctioned off to buy war bonds.

Red Cross nurses and volunteers look snappy as they march proudly down Main Street during a World War II Memorial Day parade.

Mr. and Mrs. Vincenzo Tulipani saw their five sons go off to war; fortunately, all five returned unharmed. From left to right are John, Aldo, Joseph, Alfred, and Albert.

Bowling has always been a popular sport in New England, and never more so than in Ridgefield. The Congregational Church purchased the old Ridgefield Club in 1917, and it was used for social activities, including bowling, for many years. One of the two alleys is pictured above.

The post office had its own bowling team back in the 1950s. From left to right are as follows:, (kneeling) Ralph Gay, and Richard Venus; (standing) Joe Wojnar, Jack Pribulo, Jack Hughes, and Eno Anderson. When the local alleys closed down the teams would travel to Wilton, Danbury, and Brewster until the Girolmettis built Ridge Bowl in 1964.

This Frank Gordon photograph, taken in 1949, shows the ladies bowling league of Ridgefield out on the town. The ladies bowled at both the Congregational Church alleys and the Ridgefield Bowling Lanes, which were located behind Bissell's Drug Store. (Korker Archives.)

A popular place to gather was the soda fountain at Bissell's Drug Store. Fred Romeo is ready to pour a glass of "Moxie," and behind him are "Squash" Travaglini, who later moved across the street and became the "Squash" of the Ridgefield News Store, and Johnny Gunn, the pharmacist. The man at the counter wearing a fedora is a salesman.

Tornadoes are relatively rare in New England, but in July 1950, one blew through Ridgefield with a vengeance. Carving out a mile long swath of destruction along Main and Governor Streets, giant trees were uprooted and power lines were downed. The damage was especially heavy on the Community Center grounds. (Korker Archives.)

The twister continued east on Governor Street, bringing destruction along the way. Part of the roof on the high school on East Ridge was blown off, causing $50,000 worth of damage. Frank Gordon, a local photographer whose shop on Main Street was bought by Clarence Korker, took these photos. (Korker Archives.)

In 1958, Ridgefield celebrated the 250th anniversary of the founding of the town. Day-long activities included a parade with bands swinging down Main Street, an outdoor pageant, religious observances, and the unveiling of a plaque on Settlers Rock that can still be seen today.

Route 7, south of New Road, hasn't changed much in the past 50 years. No new highway has replaced the two-lane road that follows the path of the Norwalk River. Except for the small shop on the right, which is gone, the other two buildings look the same. (C.F. Korker, Korker Archives.)

One of the few fast food restaurants in the area in the 1950s and '60s was the Ridgefield Diner on Route 7 near the Danbury line. The building is still in use, but has been the home of Ridgefield European Motors for 25 years. (C.F. Korker, Korker Archives.)

In 1959, construction was underway for the new Donnelly Plaza shopping center off Governor Street, the first large-scale construction project of its kind in Ridgefield. To follow within the coming decade were Copps Hill Plaza, Casagmo and Fox Hill garden apartments, four elementary schools, and a new high school. The face of Ridgefield was changing. (C.F. Korker, Korker Archives.)

ACKNOWLEDGMENTS

The drawings and photographs reproduced in this book reflect life as it has been lived in Ridgefield for almost 300 years. There was a wealth of material from which to choose, especially from the period between 1880 and 1960. We thank the organizations that lent photographs from their archives, and the many individuals who searched through their own collections for images from the past. We're sorry we couldn't use every photograph submitted, but space limitations made it impossible. Without your help this book would not have been possible, and we thank you.

Nano and Carol Ancona
Hersam Press
Bacchiochi Photo Service
Ferdinand Bedini and Wendy Erich
Aldo Biagiotti
Walter Boyce
Yole Casagrande
Roy Cogswell
Olga Bellagamba Cohen
Elsie Fossi Craig
Helen Cumming
Dominic D'Addario
Housing Authority of Ridgefield

Jerusalem Lodge, #49, AF&AM
Keeler Tavern Museum
Joy Kluess
Paul Korker, Korker Studios
Carol Mitchell
Abraham Morelli
Andrew Morelli
Phyllis Paccadolmi
Mary Paterniani
Delphine Giardini Pierandri
Ridgefield Community Center
Ridgebury Congregational
    Church

Mrs. Paul Rosa
David Scott, Architect
Jack Sanders
Stephen Tobin
Aldo Tulipani
Joseph Tulipani
Lolly Dunworth Turner
Richard Venus
Mrs. David P. Watson
Mrs. Joseph Wittman, Jr.
Weir Farm National Historic Site

Another special thank you must go the volunteers of the **RIDGEFIELD ARCHIVES COMMITTEE**, who have spent hundreds of hours doing all of the things it takes to get a book published. We've learned so much along the way, and have had fun doing it. We hope you will enjoy this look into our heritage.

Kay Ables, Chairman
Nancy Boersma
Ann Buccitti
Elise Haas

Helen Lewis
Robert Pokorak
Anne Quackenbush
Jack Sanders

Patricia Stephens
Jeanne Timpanelli
Richard Venus
Walter Voight